Contents

Any words appearing in the text in bold, **like this,** are explained in the Glossary.

What is the Sun?

The Sun is a star, just like those we can see twinkling at night. It looks much bigger and brighter because it is much closer to us than the other stars. The Sun is 150 million kilometres (93 million miles) away from us. The next closest star after the Sun is 270,000 times further away! If you could travel billions of kilometres out into space and look back at our Sun, you would see just a tiny star, like all the other stars.

The Sun is an ordinary star, like many of the others we can see in the sky at night.

THE UNIVERSE

The Sun

Revised and Updated

Dr Raman K. Prinja

Heinemann

www.heinemann.co.uk/library
Visit our website to find out more information about Heinemann Library books.

To order:
 Phone 44 (0) 1865 888066
 Send a fax to 44 (0) 1865 314091
 Visit the Heinemann Bookshop at www.heinemann.co.uk/library to browse our catalogue and order online.

First published in Great Britain by Heinemann, Halley Court, Jordan Hill, Oxford, OX2 8EJ, part of Pearson Education.
Heinemann is a registered trademark of Pearson Education Ltd.

Editorial: Nick Hunter and Rachel Howells
Design: Richard Parker and Manhattan Design
Illustrations: Art Construction
Picture Research: Mica Brancic
Production: Julie Carter

Originated by Modern Age
Printed in China by Leo Paper Group

ISBN 9780431154664 (hardback)
11 10 09 08 07
10 9 8 7 6 5 4 3 2 1

ISBN 9780431154794 (paperback)
12 11 10 09 08
10 9 8 7 6 5 4 3 2 1

British Library Cataloguing in Publication Data
Prinja, Raman, 1961-
The Sun. - 2nd ed. - (The universe)
1. Sun - Juvenile literature
I. Title
523.7

A full catalogue record for this book is available from the British Library.

Acknowledgements
The Publishers would like to thank the following for permission to reproduce photographs: Astrophoto p. 4; Getty Images p. 5; NASA pp. 10, 15 (top and bottom), 16, 23; NHPA p. 8; Phil Cooke and Magnet Harlequin p. 7; Photodisc p. 9; Science Photo Library pp. 11, 12, 13, 17, 19, 20, 21, 25, 26, 27, 28, 29.

Cover photograph reproduced with permission of Science Photo Library/Detlev Van Ravenswaay.

The publishers would like to thank Geza Gyuk of the Adler Planetarium, Chicago, for his assistance in the preparation of this book.

Every effort has been made to contact copyright holders of any material reproduced in this book. Any omissions will be rectified in subsequent printings if notice is given to the publishers.

The Sun, as we see it from Earth, looks yellow.

The Sun is just one star in a collection of about 100 billion stars that make up our **galaxy**, called the Milky Way. In a galaxy like ours, the stars are held together by **gravity** in a magnificent spiral pattern. The Sun lies well away from the centre of the Milky Way and is a very ordinary star. There are many stars in our galaxy that are hundreds of times bigger, and millions of times more powerful. However, the Sun is the most important to us because without it life on Earth would not exist.

A giant ball of hot gas

The Sun is a huge ball of hot, glowing gases. It is by far the brightest object seen in the sky. From Earth, the Sun appears yellow, but if you were in space or on the Moon, the Sun would look white. This is because some parts of the Sun's white light are removed when it passes through Earth's **atmosphere**. The remaining colours appear yellow.

As Earth turns on its **axis** different parts of the planet turn to face the Sun. This is why we get day and night. Standing on Earth, it looks as if the Sun is moving across the sky during the day. Really it is Earth that is spinning, and making the Sun appear to rise in the east and set in the west.

This movement also makes the shadows cast by sunlight long in the morning and evening, but short at midday. Through the ages **sundials** have been used to tell the time of day using the length and direction of shadows.

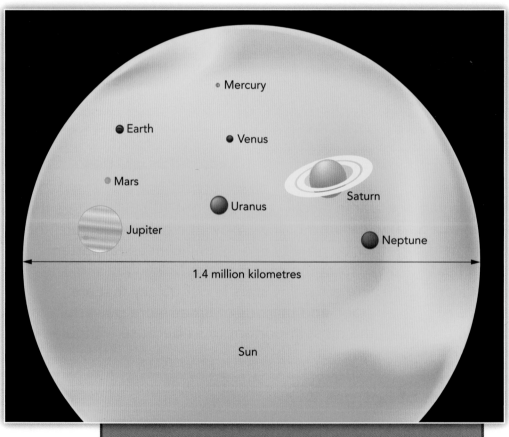

The Sun is much larger than all the planets in the solar system. The relative sizes of the planets are not exactly to scale.

The Sun and the solar system

The Sun is the largest object in the **solar system**. The planets, moons, **asteroids**, and **comets** are other members of the solar system. The Sun is 109 times larger than Earth. You could fit a million planets the size of Earth inside a hollow ball the size of the Sun. It is 700 times heavier than all of the planets in our solar system put together. That means the Sun has a very strong **gravity** that keeps all the planets **orbiting** around it. If the Sun was not there, the planets would glide away into space.

The Sun god Ra was usually painted in human form, with a falcon head.

What did people think of the Sun in the past?

The Sun was very important to people in the past. It still plays a special part in art, music and religion today. Many ancient civilizations worshipped some type of Sun god. More than 3,000 years ago, in ancient Egypt the Sun god was known as Ra. The Egyptians believed Ra created the world, and had two children who became the **atmosphere** and the clouds on Earth. Almost 1,000 years later, the ancient Greeks believed that the Sun was the chariot of the god Helios. The chariot was driven across the heavens by four horses. Later, the Romans believed Apollo was the Sun god of light.

Life on Earth depends on the Sun. It gives us light and warmth.

We depend on the Sun

The Sun supports life on Earth by giving us light, warmth, and helping the plants we use as food to grow. The Sun's power also gives us seasons and changes our weather. Some of the fuels we use to make electricity come from plants and animals that lived millions of years ago. These plants and animals also depended on the Sun for life. When the living things died, they were slowly broken down inside Earth to make **fossil fuels** such as coal and oil.

The Sun's heat turns some of the water from lakes and oceans into **vapour**, which rises into the air. This water vapour then cools and falls as the rain that plants need to grow. This process is called the **water cycle**. Plants also use the Sun's rays to turn water and **carbon** dioxide gas into food (glucose) and oxygen that we need to breathe. This process is called **photosynthesis**. Without the Sun, there would be no life on Earth.

Stonehenge

Throughout history humans have sometimes placed large stones on the ground in careful patterns. Today we believe many of these were monuments to the Sun. Stonehenge in England could be one example. It was built almost 5,000 years ago. Thirty very tall stones were arranged in a large circle. The ancient people might have used the giant stones to celebrate the time of year by watching the Sun and Moon rise and set behind these stones.

Does the Sun always stay the same?

Looking up at clear blue skies, you might think that the Sun never changes. It seems like a calm, glowing, yellow ball giving a steady stream of warmth and light. However, there is much more to the Sun than meets the eye. Just as Earth's weather is sometimes stormy, there can also be extremely violent and powerful storms on the Sun.

Powerful explosions and giant eruptions are seen in this picture of the Sun taken from space.

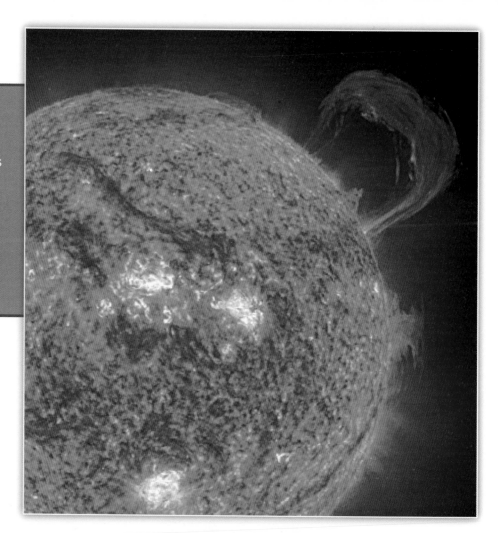

Powerful explosions

Enormous explosions called **flares** are sometimes seen on the Sun. The gas inside a flare can have a temperature of more than 1 million°Celsius (1.8 million°Fahrenheit). If we could trap the energy from just one large flare, it would be 100 million times greater than the energy released by a **volcano** exploding on Earth.

This picture was taken using a spacecraft called *SOHO*. It shows huge amounts of gas streaming away from the Sun and spreading out into the **solar system**. The bright Sun itself has been blocked out – the white circle marks it.

Giant eruptions

Another sign of a very stormy Sun is when huge bubbles of gas are thrown out into the **solar system**. A big eruption can send more than 10 billion tonnes of gas travelling very fast into space.

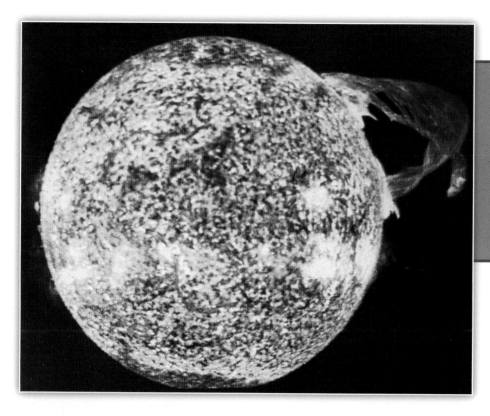

This huge loop of gas above the Sun's surface is called a **prominence**.

How can explosions on the Sun affect us?

The material blown off from the Sun during a storm is **electrically charged**. It can cause a huge amount of electricity to enter the Earth's **magnetic field**, bending it and causing it to shake violently. The **particles** arriving from the Sun can cause problems with radio and television signals. **Satellites orbiting** Earth could stop working, and there can even be power cuts in our cities. Because of this link between the stormy Sun and the Earth, scientists keep a close eye on the weather in space.

Striking our planet Earth

When material from the Sun causes the Earth's magnetic field to shake it can make some of the electrical particles enter the Earth's **atmosphere**. Bright flashes of light appear when these electric particles slam into the upper parts of Earth's atmosphere. We can sometimes see these displays as dazzling dances of green, blue, white, and red light in the night sky. These are known as Aurora Borealis (or northern lights) and Aurora Australis (or southern lights). The aurorae are most often seen from places close to the North **Pole**, like Alaska, or near the South Pole, like Antarctica.

This dazzling Aurora Borealis was photographed in the night sky over Manitoba, Canada.

What is the Sun made of?

Like Earth, the Sun is made of many different layers. However, unlike Earth, the Sun's layers are all made of incredibly hot gas. The gas is mostly hydrogen and some helium.

The core at the centre of the Sun is surrounded by hot gases.

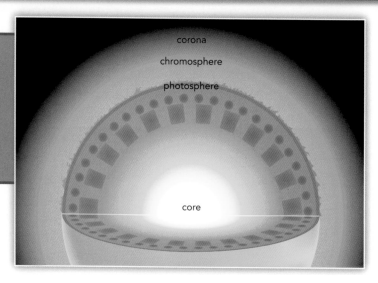

Layers that we can see from Earth

The Sun has three outer layers that we can see from Earth.

The outside layer is called the **corona**. The temperature here is over 1 million°Celsius (1.8 million°Fahrenheit) and the gas is very thinly spread. The wispy material in the corona can extend millions of kilometres into space.

The layer below the corona is called the **chromosphere**. It is about 2,000 kilometres (1,250 miles) thick and is made of hydrogen gas. It can have a temperature of around 10,000°Celsius (18,000°Fahrenheit). Violent eruptions can often be seen exploding into the chromosphere. Beautiful loops of glowing gas called **prominences** are sometimes lifted up hundreds of thousands of kilometres above the surface of the Sun (see photo on page 12).

The lowest layer we can see is called the **photosphere**. It is 300 kilometres (185 miles) thick and has a temperature of 5,500°Celsius (9,900°Fahrenheit). Nearly all the bright sunlight we get on Earth comes from the photosphere. Sometimes dark patches called sunspots can be seen on this layer. Sunspots appear dark because they are cooler and more **magnetic** than the surrounding regions of the Sun.

2003/10/28 06:24 UT

Dark patches called sunspots are seen on the Sun in this picture. Some of these groups of spots are around 20 times larger than Earth.

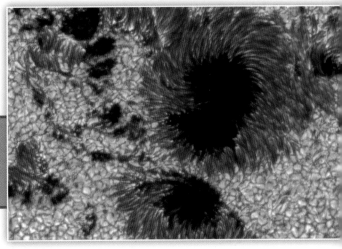

This is a close-up picture of a sunspot.

The Sun's core

At the centre of the Sun there is an incredibly hot region called the **core**. We cannot see into the core but scientists think its temperature is about 14 million°Celsius (about 25 million°Fahrenheit). We will see in the next chapter that this is where the Sun's power and energy comes from.

What makes the Sun shine?

The Sun gives off a lot of energy, and this is what makes it shine. If we could gather all the energy given off by the Sun in just one second, it would give the people of Europe all the electricity they need for the next 10 million years! All this energy is made in the **core** or centre of the Sun.

An amazing power station

Like most of the stars in our **galaxy**, the Sun is made mostly of hydrogen gas. In the core of the Sun this gas is incredibly hot. It is 14 million°Celsius (25 million°Fahrenheit) and the gas is very tightly squeezed together by the Sun's strong **gravity**.

In the incredible heat and pressure, atoms of hydrogen are brought together and fused into a different gas called helium. When this happens energy is given off. This change is called **nuclear fusion**.

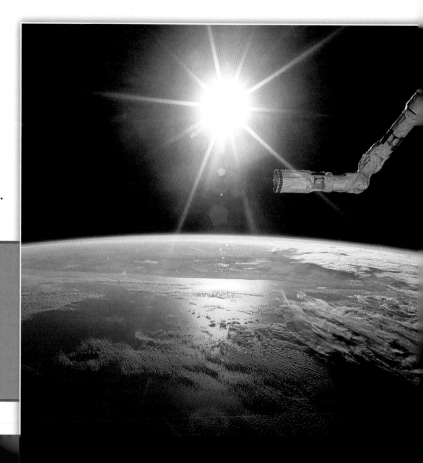

A bright Sun is seen against a dark sky from space. Astronauts on the Space Shuttle took this picture.

This picture shows the power and fury of the Sun. Huge loops of very hot gas swirl and arch over the surface of the Sun. The enormous energy comes from the core of the Sun.

The Sun gets all its energy from nuclear fusion. Today, and every day, the Sun is changing 700 million tonnes of hydrogen into 695 million tonnes of helium every second. The 5 million tonnes that are left over are turned into energy.

The energy from the core slowly works its way out. When it reaches the Sun's outer layer, called the **photosphere**, we can see it as brilliant sunshine. On Earth, we receive the energy from the Sun as heat and light.

What causes a solar eclipse?

The Sun is at the centre of the **solar system**. Earth moves around the Sun in an **orbit** that takes one year to complete. As Earth glides around the Sun, the Moon orbits around Earth about once every month. The motion of the Moon around Earth, and Earth around the Sun can sometimes lead to special events called **eclipses**.

A **solar** eclipse (or eclipse of the Sun) is one of the most amazing events in space that we can watch from Earth. It happens when the Moon passes directly between Earth and the Sun, and blocks out the Sun's light. This only happens about once every two years. It is rare because all three have to be in exactly the right places.

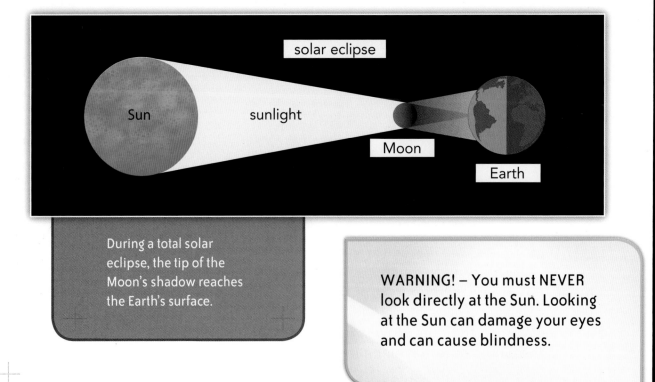

solar eclipse

Sun   sunlight

Moon

Earth

During a total solar eclipse, the tip of the Moon's shadow reaches the Earth's surface.

WARNING! – You must NEVER look directly at the Sun. Looking at the Sun can damage your eyes and can cause blindness.

During a total eclipse most of the Sun's light is totally blocked by the Moon, but not all eclipses are total. When the Moon only covers a part of the Sun, some of the sunlight can get through. This is called a partial eclipse.

How can a tiny Moon block out a huge Sun?

Although the Sun is 400 times larger than the Moon, the Moon looks exactly the same size as the Sun in our skies. This is because the Sun is 400 times further away from us than the Moon. This is why the Moon can cover the whole Sun in a total eclipse.

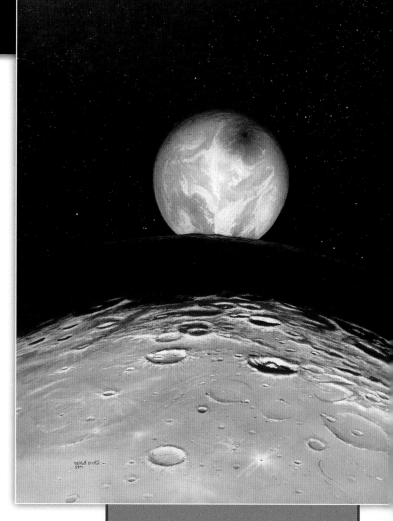

This is a view of Earth, from space, during a total solar eclipse. The people who live where the Moon's shadow is hitting Earth will be able to see the eclipse.

Try it for yourself

To see how a solar eclipse works, get someone tall to stand a few metres away. Then notice how you can hold up your thumb close to your eyes and block out (or eclipse) the person.

The greatest show on Earth

During a **solar eclipse** the shadow of the Moon falls over only a small area on Earth. The darkest part of the shadow is never more than a few hundred kilometres wide. If you are lucky enough to be in the right part of the world and standing in this shadow, you will see the Sun's face completely hidden behind the Moon. It is a fantastic sight as the Moon moves slowly across the Sun.

Just before the Sun is completely covered up by the Moon, it can only shine through a few valleys between mountains on the Moon. This lovely sight is called Bailey's beads. A few seconds later, only one light beam shines through, making the Sun look like a brilliant diamond ring.

This beautiful 'diamond ring' effect is seen just before the Sun's light is blocked out by the Moon.

The most beautiful part of a total eclipse lasts only a few minutes. This is how long the Sun is completely hidden behind the Moon. The midday sky goes almost as dark as night. Bright stars can be seen, birds stop singing, flowers begin to close, and it gets colder. In the sky you can see the amazing pearly white light of the Sun's **corona**. It shimmers around the outside of the Moon.

The Sun is now completely hidden behind the Moon. At this time, the amazing white light of the corona can be seen.

What did ancient people think of a solar eclipse?

Long ago, people were frightened by how the light of day became night in the middle of the day during an eclipse. The word *eclipse* comes from a Greek word meaning "abandonment". To abandon something means to leave it behind. They thought the Sun was abandoning Earth.

The Chinese people thought an invisible dragon or demon was eating the Sun. They would bang on pots and drums to make a loud noise during an eclipse, to frighten the dragon away. In India people would dip themselves up to the neck in water. They thought this act of worship would help frighten off the demon. In Japan people once believed that poison dropped from the sky during an eclipse, so they covered up all their drinking wells.

Will the Sun last forever?

The Sun will shine steadily for a very long time, but not forever. All stars live and die. These changes are very slow and happen over billions of years.

Today, our Sun is already middle-aged. It has enough hydrogen in its **core** to carry on shining for another 5 billion years. After that time, there will be no hydrogen left to make energy to keep the Sun going. This will be a time for major changes.

A red giant Sun

Thousands of years after its hydrogen fuel has run out, the Sun's outer layers will expand outward like a giant balloon. This is because of extra heat coming out of the core. At this point the Sun will become a **red giant** star. It will swell into hundreds of times the size it is today and turn red. The Sun will be so large that it will swallow up the planets Mercury and Venus.

This diagram shows the size of the Sun today compared to the size it will be when it becomes a bloated red giant star, 5 billion years from now.

red giant star

Sun

The death of the Sun

The outer layers of the Sun will then move far away from the star. A huge shell of gas will be shed by the Sun, peeling away nearly half of its material. This material will form an enormous cloud, which will grow much larger than the whole **solar system**. These clouds are called **planetary nebulae**. When the Sun sheds a planetary nebula it will be a sign that its death is very near.

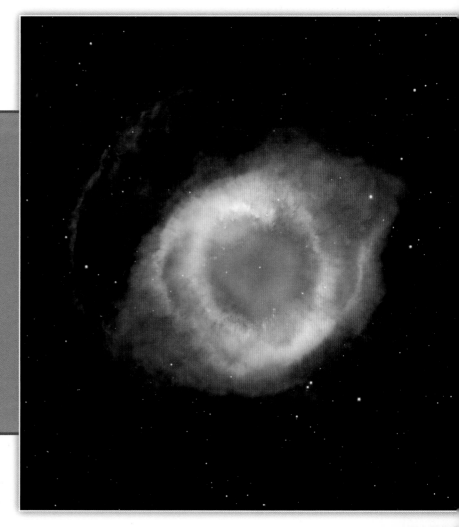

This planetary nebula is many billions of kilometres away from us. A dying star has puffed away its outer layers of gas. The Sun will shed a planetary nebula like this after it has turned into a red giant star.

Gravity rules

The force of **gravity** is always trying to crush the Sun. The energy made from **nuclear fusions** helps the Sun push outwards to stop the squeeze of gravity. When the hydrogen fuel finally runs out, there won't be enough energy to stop the force of gravity. Gravity will win, and the **core** will get crushed into a ball the size of Earth.

After the **planetary nebula** has been puffed away into space, all that will be left is a tiny, hot, tightly squeezed core. This is called a **white dwarf**. It starts off nearly 100,000°Celsius (180,000° Fahrenheit), and it is made of very tightly packed **carbon** material. There is nothing like it on Earth. If you could bring a teaspoon of white dwarf material to Earth, it would weigh 5 tonnes! Over billions of years the white dwarf will cool down into a cold, dark object that doesn't give off any light at all.

The Sun will end its life as a tiny white dwarf star. It will become much smaller than it is today.

Sun

White dwarf

Earth

This painting shows what the Sun might look like from Mars when it becomes a red giant star.

What will happen to Earth?

About 5 billion years from now, when the Sun is a **red giant**, it will be more than 200 times its present size. Earth will just barely escape being swallowed up. There will be a huge, red Sun covering almost a third of our sky.

The fierce heat from the huge Sun will slowly scorch our planet's **atmosphere**. The heat will burn all the plants and animals, and boil away the oceans. The temperature on the surface of Earth will be a sizzling 1,000°Celsius (1,800° Fahrenheit). All life on Earth will come to an end, but don't panic, the death of the Sun, and burning of the Earth, is billions of years away.

How do we learn about the Sun?

Scientists study the Sun because it is very important for life on Earth. The Sun can also teach us about the billions of other stars in our **galaxy**. There are 3 main ways that scientists learn about the Sun:

Using eclipses

Only during a total **eclipse** of the Sun can the dazzling outer part of the Sun called the **corona** be seen easily. At other times, the light from the Sun's **photosphere** is so bright that it totally outshines the corona. So scientists take pictures and carry out many experiments during an eclipse. They are trying to find out why the corona is so hot.

Using telescopes

Far more light reaches Earth from the Sun than from any other star. **Astronomers** use telescopes to study the light from the Sun. They find out about the Sun's temperature and **magnetic field**, and also about the different chemicals in its layers.

The largest telescope in the world to study the Sun is the McMath solar telescope in Arizona, USA. The telescope tower is over 30 metres tall.

Using spacecraft

We learn most about the Sun by using special telescopes that are launched into space. These powerful instruments are sent on spacecraft and they give the best pictures of the Sun. One of these spacecraft is called *Ulysses*. It was the first ever spacecraft to fly 200 million kilometres (124 million miles) above the North and South **Poles** of the Sun. Another spacecraft called *SOHO* was launched in December 1995. It has sent back amazing pictures of explosions on the Sun. The *Genesis* mission, launched in 2001, collected samples of the **solar** "wind" and brought them back to Earth.

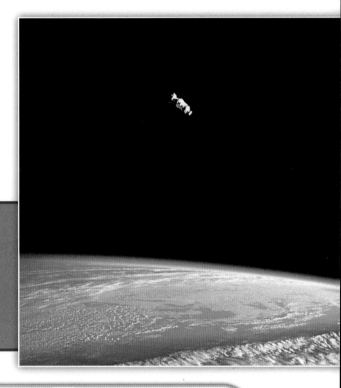

The *Ulysses* spacecraft is seen here floating above the Earth. It was launched into space in October 1990 to study the Sun.

Could I ever visit the Sun?

You could never visit the Sun because most of it is much too hot. There is also no solid place to land on; it is a gigantic ball of glowing gas. To fly anywhere near the Sun you would need a spacecraft that can stand temperatures of thousands of degrees Celsius. Humans could not survive the enormous heat and light from the Sun. After all, even at the safe distance of Earth, the Sun can harm us if we stay out in its rays for too long.

Fact File

Here are some interesting facts about the Sun:

Size – The Sun is about 1.4 million kilometres (860,000 miles) across. If you think of the Sun as a basketball, then Earth would be the size of a pinhead!

Weight – The Sun is 330,000 times heavier than Earth. This means the pull of **gravity** is much stronger for the Sun. Something that weighs 35 kilograms on Earth would weigh 1 tonne on the Sun.

Distance – The Sun is 150 million kilometres (93 million miles) from Earth. If you imagine a car travelling from Earth at a speed of 80 kilometres per hour (50 miles per hour), it would take 214 years to reach the Sun!

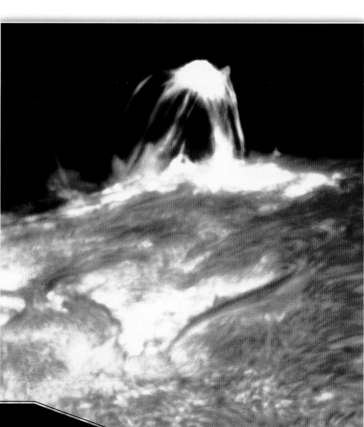

The Sun has a surface made of bubbling hot gas.

At sunset and sunrise, light from the Sun travels through much more of Earth's **atmosphere**. Some colours are removed, leaving mainly red, orange and yellow for us to see.

Temperature – The centre of the Sun has a temperature of 14 million°Celsius (25 million°Fahrenheit). The upper layer of the Sun that we can directly see is 5,500°Celsius (9,932°Fahrenheit).

Spin – The Sun spins on its **axis** about once every 25 days.

Age – The Sun is 4,600 million years old.

Brightness – The Sun is as bright as 4 trillion trillion 100-watt light bulbs. (This huge number is written as 4 followed by 24 zeros!)

Numbers
One thousand is written as 1,000. One million is 1,000,000 and one billion is 1,000,000,000.

Glossary

asteroid small, rocky object in the solar system, which moves around the Sun

astronomer scientist who studies objects in space, such as planets and stars

atmosphere layers of gases that surround a planet

axis imaginary line around which a planet or moon spins

carbon element in all living things

chromosphere outer layer of the Sun that lies between the photosphere and corona

comet small, icy object made of gas and dust, which orbits around the Sun

core central part of an object, such as a planet or star

corona extremely thin and extremely hot outermost layer of the Sun

eclipse event during which one object passes in front of another

electrically charged full of electricity

flare powerful explosions

fossil fuel natural fuel such as coal, oil, or gas

galaxy collection of billions of stars, gas and dust held together by gravity

gravity force that pulls all objects towards the surface of Earth, or any other planet, moon or star

magnetic having the power to attract or repel pieces of iron

magnetic field region of space affected by a magnetic object

nuclear fusion process where elements are joined to produce a new susbstance

orbit path taken by an object as it moves around another body (planet or star). The Moon follows an orbit around Earth.

particle tiny amount, or piece, of a substance

photosphere layer of the Sun from which most of the light escapes

photosynthesis process by which green plants make their food using energy from the Sun

planetary nebula cloud of gas seen surrounding stars like the Sun when they run out of energy and begin to die

Poles points due North and South that mark the ends of an invisible line, called the axis, about which a planet, moon or star spins

prominence huge loop of gas that erupts from the Sun

red giant star that has swollen to a much larger size than the Sun is today

satellite object that revolves around a larger body (planet or star). Satellites can be natural, such as the Moon, or man-made.

solar to do with the Sun

solar system group of eight planets and other objects orbiting the Sun

sundial instrument that shows the time of day by using the shadow cast by sunlight

vapour the gas state of a liquid

volcano opening in a planet's surface through which hot liquid rock is thrown up

water cycle movement of water all around us. Heat from the Sun boils away some water from the rivers, lakes and oceans to form clouds. Rain falls from the clouds and returns the water to the rivers, lakes and oceans.

white dwarf very hot and small object that forms when stars like the Sun run out of energy and die

More books to read

Sun, Robin Birch (Chelsea House Publications, 2004)
The Sun, Darlene R. Stille (Child's World, 2003)
The Sun is a Star, Kate Petty (Franklin Watts, 2003)

Index